Finish

(c

To be...

Beware the Ides...

Something wicked...

Full of sound and Fury...

Cry "Havoc!"

When in disgrace ...

A Horse! A Horse!...

O Romeo! Romeo!...

Friends, Romans...

Perchance to dream...

Tomorrow and Tomorrow ...

Now is the winter...

Lord, what fools...

FORWARD

Shakespeare's Hundred Best One-Liners was conceived with modest intent of seductively wetting the appetite of the Shakespeare-challenged and luring Bard dropouts back to the fold. Hopefully, even this minimal exposure will inspire both groups to "screw their courage to the sticking place;" and, make that rewarding plunge into the boundless seas of Shakespeare's timeless plays and poetry.

As a bonus, if any of these raw "to be or not to be" recruits should have the misfortune of finding themselves collared by a Shakespearean bombast, they will be verbally forearmed to zap him with one of the Bard's admonitions, "Speak less than thou knowest."

Shakespeare's
Hundred Best One-Liners

(Winnowed and Interpolated)

by

Jack W. Thomas

Dedicated to our one-of-a kind high school drama teacher

LLOYD E. ROBERTS

Cover design and illustration: Norman Kingford Vance
Text design and typeset: Carol L. Delattre

Manufactured in the United States of America

Shakespeare's Hundred Best One-liners
is distributed and Published by:

Corporate Towers
Post Office Box 282
Malibu, CA 90265

ISBN 09674779-0-5
Library of Congress Catalog Number
First Edition

Printed in the United States of America

Plus: Fifty of Shakespeare's words or phrases that have survived over 400 years and are still in use today as; Household Words.

Number One: Household Words

"Household words"

King Henry V, Act IV

Table of Contents

Sampler

"Saint-seducing gold."

Romeo and Juliet, Act I

Interpolation:

This cynical assessment of man's innate greed would have us believe that St. Francis himself would gladly serve up his favorite dove for the devil's lunch if sufficient gold were heaped at his feet.

"Wisely and slow; they stumble that run fast."

Romeo and Juliet, Act II

Interpolation:

Advance judiciously lest you spend the better part of your life picking yourself up.

Number Two: Household words

"Salad Days"

Antony and Cleopatra, Act I

"Delays have dangerous ends."

King Henry VI, Part I, Act III

Interpolation:

Shakespeare lived only 52 years. Yet in that time he produced forty-two plays. It must be acknowledged that he was not given to procrastination. To put off any task will, in the end, only serve to exacerbate the problem, never solve it.

"Do not give dalliance Too much the rein."

The Tempest, Act IV

Interpolation:

If you give your horse or dalliance too much rein, both will all too happily deliver you to a destination of their choosing.

Number Three: Household Words

"Bated Breath"

Merchant of Venice, Act I

"Tempt not a desperate man."

Romeo and Juliet, Act V

Interpolation:

Desperation can turn even the most civilized man into a fearsome savage.

"How poor are they that have not patience! What wound did ever heal but by degrees?"

Othello, Act II

Interpolation:

Rub with soothing balms, anoint with healing salves: for all your doctoring wounds of the flesh (or psyche) respond more frequently and readily to the calendar, not the apothecary.

Number Four: Household Words
"The Naked Truth"
Love's Labour's Lost, Act V

Lies

"Lord, Lord, how this world is given to lying!"

King Henry IV, Part I, Act V

Interpolation:

Oh, God! Please rid this world of the mendacious.

"To be honest, as this world goes, is to be one man picked out of ten thousand."

Hamlet, Act II

Interpolation:

With the Bard as bookmaker the odds of finding an honest man stand at ten thousand to one.

Number Five: Household Words

"Good Riddance"

Troilus and Cressida, Act II

"Let me have no lying; it becomes none but tradesmen."

The Winter's Tale, Act IV

Interpolation:

It would seem that shopkeepers and merchants in Shakespeare's day had a well-known propensity for prevarication.

"This above all: to thine own self be true, and it must follow, as the night the day, thou canst not then be false to any man."

Hamlet, Act I

Interpolation:

Truly honest persons cannot lie to anyone including themselves.

Number Six: Household Words

"Dead as a doornail"

King Henry VI, Part 2, Act IV

"You lie in your throat."

King Henry IV, Part II, Act I

Interpolation:
A stinging challenge.

Women

"The pleasing punishment that women bear."

The Comedy of Errors, Act I

Interpolation:

At times the uninhibited act of love-making approaches the intensity of combat: but the punishment endured can also be most pleasing.

Number Seven: Household Words

"Hoodwinked"

All's Well That End's Well, Act IV

"There was never yet fair woman but she made mouths in a glass."

King Lear, Act III

Interpolation:

How shallow are those self-indulgent lives that are whiled away admiring alabaster complexions and swan-long necks in omnipresent mirrors.

"The ripest fruit first falls."

King Richard II, Act II

Interpolation:

The most desirable and sweetest are always the first to be plucked.

Number Eight: Household Words

"Star-crossed lovers"

Romeo and Juliet, Prologue

"Everything that grows Holds in perfection but a little moment."

Sonnet 15

Interpolation:

Never again will the spring's first roses bud, the two-year-old mare, nor this season's debutante exude that ephemeral beauty of youth.

"Thou art thy mother's glass, and she in thee calls back the lovely April of her prime."

Sonnet 3

Interpolation:

When a mother looks at her daughter she cannot help but reflect upon her own past, those days of wine and roses.

Number Nine: Household Words

"The Green-Eyed Monster"

Othello, Act III

"She's beautiful and therefore to be wooed, She is a woman, therefore to be won."

King Henry VI, Part I, Act V

Interpolation:

If a woman is beautiful she has no doubt been wooed ardently, and by many; only the most determined and forceful suitor will contrive to bed her.

"The lady doth protest too much, methinks."

Hamlet, Act III

Interpolation:

"No" said too vehemently and frequently risks being misconstrued as a yes.

Number Ten: Household Words

"Milk of human kindness"

Macbeth, Act I

"Do you not know I am a woman? when I think, I must speak."

As You Like It, Act III

Interpolation:

Every banal thought that scurries through this woman's mind must be articulated. Has Shakespeare been dead long enough to escape being branded a chauvinist?

"Great with child, and longing. . . for stewed prunes."

Measure for Measure, Act II

Interpolation:

Today pregnant mothers send their husbands out for pickles and ice cream. In the 16th century the placebo of choice was stewed prunes.

Number Eleven: Household Words

"Stood on ceremonies"

Julius Caesar, Act II

"'Tis the strumpet's plague to beguile many and be beguiled by one."

Othello, Act IV

Interpolation:

No matter how skillful a woman is in attracting and satisfying lovers there is always one predictably unattainable dandy or gigolo in her life that she is smitten by, but cannot charm.

Number Twelve: Household Words
"Good night, ladies;"
Hamlet, Act IV

Death

"To be, or not to be: that is the question:"

Hamlet, Act III

Interpolation:

One of the most famous lines in all literature. We each stand alone peering into a bottomless chasm and must make our individual decision: do we succumb to life's trials or overcome them?

"Tomorrow, and tomorrow, and tomorrow, creeps in this petty pace from day to day, To the last syllable of recorded time; And all our yesterdays have lighted fools The way to dusty death. Out, out, brief candle!"

Macbeth Act V

Interpolation:

Life stretches out before each of us to the end of our own personal eternity. It inchworms by until our last tomorrow inexorably snuffs out the flickering candle that eliminated all our yesterdays.

Number Thirteen: Household Words

"What's past is prologue"

The Tempest Act II

"Golden lads and girls all must, as chimney-sweepers, come to dust."

Cymbeline, Act IV

Interpolation:

No one escapes, the lame, the halt, the blind and the beautiful are condemned to the same end.

**"Of comfort no man speak:
Let's talk of graves,
of worms, and epitaphs;
Make dust our paper,
and with rainy eyes write
sorrow on the bosom of the
earth; let's choose
executors and talk of wills."**

King Richard II, Act III

Interpolation:

When that unpleasant yet inevitable time comes to stand face to face with death, we must avoid circumlocution and hyperbole: worms, epitaphs, executors, and wills should dominate the conversation.

Number Fourteen: Household Words

"Neither rhyme nor reason"

The Comedy of Errors, Act II

"Imperious Caesar, dead and turned to clay, Might stop a hole to keep the wind away."

Hamlet, Act V

Interpolation:

Conquer the world, have Cleopatra at your feet, yet one day your earthly residue might do no more than stop a hole in a wall to buffer the wind.

"Cowards die many times before their deaths; The valiant never taste of death but once."

Julius Caesar, Act II

Interpolation:

Cowards must face the anticipated agony of death again and again, and yet again. Not so the brave man.

Number Fifteen: Household Words

"Devil incarnate"

King Henry V, Act II

"A man may fish with the worm that hath eat of a king, and eat of a fish that hath fed of that worm."

Hamlet, Act IV

Interpolation:

Life is a cycle. The worm eats the king and we use that very worm to catch the fish that will serve as our royal dinner.

"Fear no more the heat o' the sun, Nor the furious winter's rages; Thou thy worldly task hast done, Home art gone, and ta'en thy wages."

Cymbeline, Act IV

Interpolation:

Neither the scorching sun nor the raw chill of winter can harm you further. What good or harm you might have done has been done. The time has come to rest.

Number Sixteen: Household Words

"The rest is silence"

Hamlet, Act V

"The end of life cancels all bands."

King Henry IV, Part I, Act III

Interpolation:

Once we have returned to dust, our enemies, bill collectors, even loved ones must release us from their enmity, judgments or affectionate doting.

"To what base uses we may return, Horatio! Why may not imagination trace the noble dust of Alexander, till he find it stopping a bung -hole?"

Hamlet, Act V

Interpolation:

If it were possible, might we not search out Alexander's noble dust and discover it stopping the bung-hole in a grease barrel?

Number Seventeen: Household Words

"Get thee to a nunnery"

Hamlet, Act III

"As flies to wanton boys, are we to the gods; They kill us for their sport."

King Lear, Act IV

Interpolation:

The gods demonstrate as little concern for we mortals as callous boys pulling wings from flies.

"The undiscovere'd country from whose bourn No traveler returns, puzzles the will And makes us rather bear those ills we have than fly to others that we know not of?"

Hamlet, Act III

Interpolation:

If but one lost soul should find his way back to recount the mysteries that lie on the other side, how many of us might willingly embark on our own journey to explore that undiscovered country?

Number Eighteen: Household Words

"A tower of strength"

King Richard III, Act V

"To die, to sleep; To sleep? perchance to dream, ay, there's the rub; For in that sleep of death what dreams may come When we have shuffled off this mortal coil, Must give us pause. There's the respect that makes calamity of so long life;"

Hamlet, Act III

Interpolation:

We endure the calamities of life fearing more the potential terror of the eternal dreams that well might await us after death.

"Full fathom five thy father lies; Of his bones are coral made: Those are pearls that were his eyes: Nothing of him that doth fade, But doth suffer a sea-change Into something rich and strange."

The Tempest, Act I

Interpolation:

A sailor's last remains lie deep in the ocean, his bones have changed to coral, his eyes to pearls. Everything about him has transmuted into something wonderfully strange.

Number Nineteen: Household Words

"Not a mouse stirring"

Hamlet, Act I

"O! that this too too solid flesh would melt, Thaw and resolve itself into a dew; Or that the Everlasting had not fixed His canon 'gainst self-slaughter! O God! O God! How weary, stale, flat, and unprofitable seem to me all the uses of this world."

Hamlet, Act I

Interpolation:

Why did God not afford us some easy way out of life? Death seems to be its sole objective while man's fleeting existence is devoid of reason, objective and is in general meritless.

"Invectives"

"You are not worth the dust which the rude wind Blows in your face."

King Lear, Act IV

Interpolation:

The small wisp of dust that is scattered to the wind when you shake a throw rug far exceeds this rascal's total worth.

Number Twenty: Household Words

"Eaten me out of house and home"

King Henry IV, Part II, Act II

"Kill thy physician, and the fee bestow Upon the foul disease."

King Lear, Act I

"The first thing we do, let's kill all the lawyers."

King Henry VI, Part II, Act IV

Interpolation:

To no one's great surprise these unkind, jaundiced views of both professions have remained constant for the last 400 years. Shakespeare's nefarious character, Dick the Butcher, who speaks this Line wants to dispatch 'all the Lawyers' as then there will be No one left to defend his future Victims.

"God made him, and therefore let him pass for a man."

Merchant of Venice, Act I

Interpolation:

Another of God's mistakes that will only stand corrected when we sing the last hymn at the ingrate's funeral.

Number Twenty-one: Household Words

"Sharper than a serpent's tooth"

King Lear, Act I

"With the help of a surgeon, he might yet recover, and prove an ass."

A Midsummer Night's Dream, Act V

Interpolation:

A highly skilled doctor might save this dolt's life to reaffirm what has long been common knowledge. The world is saddled with an oaf, blockhead, and clod.

"When he is best, he is a little worse than a man, and when he is worst, he is little better than a beast."

The Merchant of Venice, Act I

Interpolation:

When he is on his best behavior, he is still less mannered than a half-civilized person. When he is on his worst behavior, he exhibits little more couth than the lowest bred stock from the field.

Number Twenty-two: Household Words

"What a piece of work is a man"

Hamlet, Act II

"A plague o' both your houses! They have made worms' meat of me."

Romeo and Juliet, Act III

Interpolation:

May your friends plus all your kin die of the plague's racking convulsions. You have reduced me to a great green shank of festering carrion fit only for worms.

"My near'st and dearest enemy."

King Henry IV, Part I, Act III

Interpolation:

Is it not possible to glean some perverted measure of solace by nurturing a steadfast and unwavering enemy?

Number Twenty-three: Household Words

"It smells to heaven"

Hamlet, Act III

"They have a plentiful lack of wit."

Hamlet, Act II

Interpolation:

Intelligence has its lofty upper limits: while stupidity shall always remain a stagnant bottomless sump.

"I do desire we may be better strangers."

As You Like It, Act III

Interpolation:

Nothing could give me more pleasure than to endure your company with greater infrequency.

Number Twenty-four: Household Words

"Laughing-stock"

The Merry Wives of Windsor, Act III

Men

"Your tale, sir, would cure deafness."

The Tempest, Act I

Interpolation:

This crashing boor's story is so inane that it might well burrow through the broken machinery in a deaf man's ears.

"Let them hang themselves in their own straps."

Twelfth Night, Act I

Interpolation:

Let their own misdeeds serve as their tormenters, and, with luck, their executioners.

Number Twenty-five: Household Words

"The primrose path"

Hamlet, Act I

"O brave new world that has such people in't!"

The Tempest, Act V

Interpolation:

In Shakespeare's day new worlds were being discovered. As the empire rapidly grew, the arts and sciences flourished. All this progress and yet, much like today, it was a world that had <u>such</u> people in it.

"Let Hercules himself do what he may, The cat will mew and dog will have his day."

Hamlet, Act V

Interpolation:

Even when confronting the mighty, the weakest and lowest on the pecking order will occasionally prevail. Yes, every dog will have his day.

Number Twenty-six: Household Words

"As white as driven snow"

The Winter's Tale, Act IV

"Men's evil manners live in brass; their virtues we write in water."

King Henry VIII, Part III, Act IV

Interpolation:

Too often we forget a man's charities, his kindness, and malign him for a few misdeeds. A variation of this aphorism is, "The evil that men do lives after them; the good is oft interred with their bones;"

Julius Caesar, Act III

"Though I look old, yet I am strong and lusty; For in my youth I never did apply Hot and rebellious liquors in my blood."

As You Like It, Act II

Interpolation:

Four hundred years ago there was no warning label on a pint of suds. Yet, somehow, any bumpkin with one iota of common sense knew that demon rum was deleterious and life shortening.

Number Twenty-seven: Household Words

"Murder most foul"

Hamlet, Act I

"A politician ... one that would circumvent God."

Hamlet, Act V

Interpolation:

The only group of professionals with the audacity, the irreverence and unmitigated gall to attempt an end run on God.

Love

"Shall I compare thee
to a summer's day?
Thou art more lovely
and more temperate:
Rough winds do shake
the darling buds of May,
And summer's lease
hath all too short a date."

Sonnet 18

Interpolation:

You fill the very air around me like a balmy, fragrant summer's day. Sadly, summer yields to fall much too quickly.

Number Twenty-eight: Household Words

"Sweets to the sweet"

Hamlet, Act V

"Age cannot wither her, nor custom stale her infinite variety;"

Antony and Cleopatra, Act II

Interpolation:

Neither the passing years nor frivolous changes in shifting fashion can diminish her power to captivate, enamor and enthrall.

"For thy sweet love remembered such wealth brings That then I scorn to change my state with kings."

Sonnet 29

Interpolation:

The mere thought of your love showers me with more wealth than could be hoarded in any king's treasure trove.

Number Twenty-nine: Household Words

"Pomp and circumstance"

Othello, Act III

"The wounds invisible That love's keen arrows make."

As You Like It, Act III

Interpolation:

The piercing arrows of love may be unseen, but that does not render them any less painful.

"Your daughter and the Moor are now making the beast with two backs."

Othello, Act I

Interpolation:

The lovers are entwined in such passionate lovemaking that they appear to be a flailing wild mutant animal with two backs.

Number Thirty: Household Words

"The apple of her eye"

Love's Labour's Lost, Act V

Life

"No sooner met, but they looked; no sooner looked but they loved; no sooner loved but they sighed; no sooner sighed but they asked one another the reason; no sooner knew the reason but they sought the remedy."

As You Like It, Act V

Interpolation:

Instant love. Instant regret. Instant breakup.

"Life's but a walking shadow, a poor player that struts and frets his hour upon the stage, And then is heard no more; it is a tale Told by an idiot, full of sound and fury, Signifying nothing."

Macbeth, Act V

Interpolation:

The vaporous shadow we call life alternately struts or slinks across our horizon. Suddenly the drama is over and in that single pulse of time all our transgressions, tribulations and glories are rendered as meaningless as the ramblings of an idiot.

Number Thirty-one: Household Words

"Too much of a good thing"

As You Like It, Act IV

"Life is as tedious as a twice-told tale, Vexing the dull ear of a drowsy man."

King John, Act III

Interpolation:

At the exact moment you are poised to doze off for a delicious nap, someone insists on telling you a story you have heard a dozen times before. Such an unsolicited and untimely tale is an example of just how boring life can sometimes seem.

Potpourri

"Our bodies are our gardens, to the which our wills are gardeners."

Othello, Act I

Interpolation:

Clay thrown by the potter, oak hewn by the carpenter, stone set by the mason—our strength of will alone can mold our bodies into that shape it decrees.

Number Thirty-two: Household Words

"Budge an inch"

The Taming of the Shrew, Induction 12

"Have more than thou showest, Speak less than thou knowest, Lend less than thou owest."

King Lear, Act I

Interpolation:

Don't make a crass display of your possessions, don't flaunt your knowledge, and don't lend more money than you have stashed away in your piggy bank.

"Heat not a furnace for your foe so hot That it do singe yourself."

King Henry VIII, Act I

Interpolation:

Uncontrolled, unfettered rage can often inflict more injury upon oneself than one's enemy.

Number Thirty-three: Household Words

"Stony-hearted villains"

King Henry IV, Part I, Act II

"The fool doth think he is wise, but the wise man knows himself to be a fool."

As You Like It, Act V

Interpolation:

When you accept how much you don't know, you stand poised at the head of the path that might someday lead to wisdom.

"He's mad that trusts in the tameness of a wolf, a horse's health, a boy's love, or a whore's oath."

King Lear, Act III

Interpolation:

Wolves are never tame, horses rarely sound, boys seldom constant in their vows, and whores all too infrequently truthful.

Number Thirty-four: Household Words

"Till the crack of doom"

Macbeth, Act IV

"Now 'tis the spring, and weeds are shallow rooted; Suffer them now and they'll o'ergrow the garden."

King Henry VI, Part II, Act III

Interpolation:

Small problems have the amazing growth potential of compound interest. 'Tis wise to address them expeditiously.

**"Neither a borrower,
nor a lender be;
For loan oft loses both
itself and friend,
And borrowing dulls
the edge of husbandry."**

Hamlet, Act I

Interpolation:

Lending not only decreases the heft of your purse, it can also accelerate the loss of friends, while borrowing lures you into improvidence with all facets of your finances.

Number Thirty-five: Household Words

"Breathe one's last"

King Henry VI, Part III, Act V

"I were better to be eaten to death with rust than to be scoured to nothing with perpetual motion."

King Henry IV, Part II, Act I

Interpolation:

Some prefer to die peacefully ensconced in their overstuffed chairs rather than succumb in the act of chasing fame, fortune or their tails.

"Every cloud engenders not a storm."

King Henry VI, Part III, Act V

Interpolation:

A few hairs in your comb does not necessarily portend baldness by week's end. But, then again, don't stop checking.

Number Thirty-six Household Words

"Laid on with a trowel"

AS You Like It, Act I

"There is a tide in the affairs of men, Which taken at the flood, leads on to fortune; Omitted, all the voyage of their life is bound in shallows and in miseries."

Julius Caesar, Act IV

Interpolation:

If you commit all your energies, at the right time, and to a proper goal, you will never have to look back in regret. Fail to earn that degree, neglect that job, and you may find yourself becalmed as your more audacious and tenacious friends sail onward to riches and glory.

"Come not between the dragon and his wrath."

King Lear, Act I

Interpolation:

Once the dragon has sent his fiery breath in Saint George's direction, it would be ill-advised to step between the combatants.

Number Thirty-seven: Household Words

"Strange bedfellows"

The Tempest, Act II

"Adam was a gardener."

King Henry VI, Part II, Act IV

Interpolation:

The first man lived by his sweat as he honorably tilled the soil.

"Fortune brings in some boats that are not steered."

Cymbeline, Act IV

Interpolation:

Good luck will find all of us on occasion: unfortunately, for most, these occasions are far too rare.

Number Thirty-eight: Household Words

"Bag and baggage"

As You Like It, Act III

"Is it not strange that desire should so many years outlive performance?"

King Henry IV, Part II, Act II

Interpolation:

Most of us still dream of invoking the skills and passions of youth long after that sweet bird has permanently flown the coop.

"Beggars mounted run their horse to death."

King Henry VI, Part III, Act I

Interpolation:

A well-tempered sword or finely crafted violin will give service for a lifetime. If mishandled, both can be destroyed in a single day.

Number Thirty-nine Household Words

"One fell swoop"

Macbeth, Act IV

"Men of few words are the best men."

King Henry V, Part II, Act III

Interpolation:

Men who say the least often accomplish the most. Logorrhea is non-productive.

"Talkers are no good doers."

King Richard III, Act I

Interpolation:

Talking and taking action, in general, are not even distant cousins.

Number Forty: Household Words

"What the dickens"

The Merry Wives of Windsor, Act III

"Words pay no debts."

Troilus and Cressida, Act III

Interpolation:

Vows, oaths and heartfelt promises never seem to have the warm comforting feel of cash in hand.

"By and by is easily said."

Hamlet, Act III

Interpolation:

I'll pay you later, or we'll set the wedding date soon, does little to assuage a lender's or a betrothed's trepidations.

Number Forty-one: Household Words

"For goodness' sake"

King Henry VIII, Act III

"Let me take you a button-hole lower."

Love's Labour's Lost, Act V

Interpolation:
It's time we get down to bedrock.

"The jury, passing on the prisoner's life, May in the sworn twelve have a thief or two Guiltier than him they try."

Measure for Measure, Act II

Interpolation:
Is it fair or inequitable to be judged by an undetected scoundrel whose string of misdeeds may be far worse than our own?

Number Forty-two: Household Words
"The game is afoot"
King Henry IV, Part I, Act I

"He that is giddy thinks the world turns round."

The Taming of the Shrew, Act V

Interpolation:

Our personal prejudice circumscribes, defines and dictates our ultimate, always suspect, judgment.

**"The worst is not,
So long as we can say,
'"This is the worst.'"**

King Lear, Act IV

Interpolation:

If you have the strength to say, "I'm dying," don't fail to exhale on the nearest mirror before your final interment. You may discover you are not yet quite dead.

Number Forty-three: Household Words

"Foregone conclusion"

Othello, Act III

"More matter, with less art."

Hamlet, Act II

Interpolation:

Enough meaningless arpeggio, lace and frills, give us more substance! (Was the Bard prescient and foresaw modern day television?)

"Brevity is the soul of wit."

Hamlet, Act II

Interpolation:

Please! I beg you, no shaggy dog stories.

Number Forty-four: Household Words

"The time is out of joint"

Hamlet, Act I

"They that touch pitch will be defiled."

Much Ado About Nothing, Act III

Interpolation:

It is not necessary to take evil into your arms and embrace it; a mere brush with depravity can leave one besmirched.

"For there was never yet philosopher That could endure the toothache patiently."

Much Ado About Nothing, Act V

Interpolation:

In the face of genuine pain, crisp, clear reason is the first facility (even ahead of rats) to jump ship.

Number Forty-five: Household Words

"To make a virtue of necessity"

The Two Gentlemen of Verona, Act IV

"The smallest worm will turn being trodden on."

King Henry VI, Part III, Act II

Interpolation:
It can be a mistake to underestimate a squirt.

**"O! it is excellent
To have a giant's
strength;
but it is tyrannous
To use it like a giant."**

Measure for Measure, Act II

Interpolation:

Having great strength is admirable, but wielding it like a bully is always base and contemptible.

Number Forty-six: Household Words

"I have immortal longings in me"

Antony and Cleopatra, Act V

"But, O! how bitter a thing it is to look into happiness through another man's eyes!"

As You Like It, Act V

Interpolation:

It is particularly painful to observe happy, successful people enjoying their merry lives if your own attempt at finding personal contentment has eluded you.

"It [drink] provokes the desire, but it takes away the performance."

Macbeth, Act II

Interpolation:

True, alcohol can be a sexual stimulant, but, unfortunately, it also lulls the machinery required for performance into sleep mode.

Number Forty-seven: Household Words

"Unsex me here"

Macbeth, Act I

**"Society is no comfort
To one not sociable."**

Cymbeline, Act IV

Interpolation:

The matrix of society is people. If you don't like people, then you can get along swimmingly without society.

"It makes us, or it mars us."

Othello, Act V

Interpolation:

Each new day's adversity is the furnace; our characters are tempered in its blast or consumed.

Number Forty-eight: Household Words

"The be-all and the end-all"

Macbeth, Act I

"There's small choice in rotten apples."

The Taming of the Shrew, Act I

Interpolation:
Is there a freeway less traveled?

"O, how full of briers is this working-day world!"

As You Like It, Act I

Interpolation:

Remember, only the types of problems change when you rush headlong into a new field of employment: the vexation and boredom remains constant.

Number Forty-nine: Household Words
"The quality of mercy"
The Merchant of Venice, Act IV

**"A jest's prosperity
lies in the ear
Of him that hears it,
never in the tongue
Of him that makes it."**

Love's Labour's Lost, Act V

Interpolation:

A skilled comic entertains his audience only with those jokes they find humorous.

"A little fire
is quickly trodden out,
Which, being suffered,
rivers cannot quench."

King Henry VI, Part III, Act IV

Interpolation:

Raze your little mound of problems each day, or on some tomorrow they will have grown to be as tall as the highest mountain.

Number Fifty: Household Words

"Remembrance of things past"

Sonnet 30

"'Tis an ill cook that cannot lick his own fingers."

Romeo and Juliet, Act IV

Interpolation:

Avoid buying produce from a farmer unless you have seen him eat his own vegetables.

"What's in a name? That which we call a rose By any other name would smell as sweet."

Romeo and Juliet, Act II

Interpolation:

It is the thing itself that repulses or enamors us, not what place, time or linguistic chance has dictated we call it.

"Lilies that fester smell far worse than weeds."

Sonnet 94

Interpolation:

It always causes us more pain to see a noble individual toppled than a base scallywag.

"The daintiest last, to make the end most sweet."

King Richard II, Act I

The End

About the Interpolator
Jack W. Thomas

Graduate of the University of Arizona. Film credits include: Original story and co-screenplay *Embryo* starring Rock Hudson and Barbara Carrera.

While co-writing *Francis of Assisi* he worked with Director Michael Curtiz.

After a stint as a Los Angeles County probation officer, he wrote eleven Bantam Books dealing with teenage delinquents which were translated into five languages and sold a million and half copies.

Jack assisted James Cagney with his best selling autobiography, *Cagney by Cagney* (Doubleday).

Is currently interviewing discriminating publishers to release his latest novel, *Fire-rock, Live-finger.*

Apologia

Our selection of typefaces made it impossible to uniformly follow the traditional typography utilized in the quartos and folios. Our *mia culpa* to the tenth power in advance.

Forthcoming Authors in the "Bard Books" series will be:

THE HOLY BIBLE Hundred Best-One-liners
CERVANTES' Hundred Best One-liners
BALZAC'S Hundred Best One-liners
SAMUEL JOHNSON'S Hundred Best One-liners
OSCAR WILDE'S Hundred Best One-liners
OMAR KHAYYAM'S Hundred Best One-liners
MACHIAVELLI'S Hundred Best One-liners
AESOP'S Hundred Best One-liners

Finish . . .

or not to be?

Ay, there's the rub.

and tomorrow . . .

...we mortals be!

...and let slip the dogs of war

. . .wherefore art thou Romeo?

...this way comes.

...countrymen, lend me your ears:

of March.

...with fortunes and men's eyes

signifying nothing.

My kingdom for a horse!

. . .of our discontent.